26
VITAL
ISSUES

26 VITAL ISSUES

Jesus' answers to life's urgent questions

LeRoy Koopman

BAKER BOOK HOUSE
Grand Rapids, Michigan

Preface

Some issues are relevant because they are *timely;* they are currently being discussed and argued in our contemporary culture. Certainly Scripture can be of help in providing principles for such discussions.

Other issues are relevant because they are *timeless;* they touch on themes which are at the very heart of human life and faith in every generation.

The twenty-six vital issues presented in this book are in the second category. All of them originated with questions people asked Jesus more than nineteen hundred years ago, yet the answers are as revolutionary and as relevant today as they were on the day they were given by the Master.

Contents

1

Being Sure
About Jesus

*"Are you he who is to come, or shall we look
for another?" (Matt. 11:3)*

Scripture for study: Matthew 11:2-6

Was the fellow who asked this question the same
one who so boldly pointed to Jesus and said, "Be-
hold, the Lamb of God, who takes away the sin of
the world!" (John 1:29)?

He was the same fellow, all right, but circumstances had changed. John the baptizer was now
sitting in the gloom of a damp prison instead of
walking freely in the sunshine, and was finding that
the moldy prison food was even worse-tasting than
locusts and wild honey. Yet Jesus had not sent a
team of angel commandos to whisk John from his
cell. What evidence was there that Jesus was living
up to His billing?

That kind of question pops up sometimes, doesn't
it? One bright Easter morning you stood before the
congregation and confessed Jesus to be the Lamb
of God who took away the sins of your personal
world. But then a friend got terribly disfigured in a
car accident, or you got a D in math, or you were

laid off at the factory, or you gained fifteen pounds, or you started having arguments with family members. What evidence is there that Jesus is still the one to follow? Should you try another?

Jesus answered John's question by telling him that great things *were* happening, even though they were not happening to John. Blind people were seeing, lame people were walking, and the poor were hearing the gospel. Jesus was telling John to look beyond the walls of his prison cell, to try to see things from a larger perspective, to judge by fact instead of by feeling.

It's not easy, but we have to try. We have to remember that God isn't necessarily dead just because we can't seem to contact Him; that Jesus isn't necessarily a fake even though a certain church official seems to be; that God hasn't forsaken us even though we have a splitting headache.

Yes, like John, we may have to sit in the gloom awhile, wondering why things aren't working out better, but we should not look for another Messiah.

INTERPRETIVE COMMENTS

John had been imprisoned by Herod Antipas because the preacher had spoken out against him for living with Herodias, his brother's wife (Luke 3:18-20). It is clear, however, that John's greatest antagonist was not Herod, but Herodias, who eventually caused John's beheading (Matt. 14:1-12). Herod treated him well and allowed John's disciples to visit him. Thus John knew what Jesus was doing and could send messages to Him.

Notice that all the works Jesus called to John's

attention were works of mercy; none were done for the sake of displaying power. Jesus shows that His messiahship is one of love and healing rather than of bombast and harshness. John's message had been primarily one of judgment (see Luke 3:7-17), and he may have been disappointed when Jesus failed to condemn evil with the same kind of fiery enthusiasm. Jesus was far more gentle than John expected the Promised One to be.

Jesus suggested that John carefully consider the mighty works that were being done; they may not be the type expected, but they were indeed mighty works. They certainly were far beyond anything John had been able to do.

Jesus also implied that John should reread the Old Testament prophecies. Jesus' reference to the healing of the blind and lame is an allusion to Isaiah 35:5; and His reference to proclaiming good news to the poor recalls Isaiah 61:1-3. Both passages had been quoted by Jesus earlier at His inaugural sermon at Nazareth (Luke 4:16-21).

DISCUSSION QUESTIONS

1. Have you ever questioned your faith? Have you ever wondered if Jesus is really the Promised One? If so, have you been hesitant to tell anyone, believing that you were the only one who felt that way?

2. Have you ever felt, like John did, that Jesus had let you down? Have you perhaps felt that you have worked hard for Him, but in a time of financial distress or family illness He did not help you? Is it legitimate to base your faith on negative expe-

riences in your life? Is it legitimate, on the other hand, to base your faith on the positive experiences? In other words, can you base your faith solely on your experience of providence?

3. If your answer to the previous question is no, then on what do you base your faith? Reflect on the answer Jesus gave John and on Hebrews 11:1-3.

4. What is commonly the relationship between faith and feeling? How reliable are our feelings when it comes to religious matters? What ought to be the relationship between faith and feeling?

5. Why do some people, especially young people, sometimes get involved with such cults as the Unification Church and the Children of God? Is it because they have become disillusioned with Christ? Is it because they have become disillusioned with Christianity as taught in their home and church? Is it because they are attracted to some characteristic of the new group? Do you see any parallels to the situation of John the baptizer?

2

Sunday Activities

"Is it lawful to heal on the sabbath?" (Matt. 12:10)

Scripture for study: Matthew 12:9-14

Is it lawful to heal on Sunday? To call on someone who is sick? To take the family on a picnic? To visit Grandpa and Grandma? To go to the movies? To go for a ride in a car or a boat? To golf? To shop? To work in a grocery store? To cultivate corn? To play professional football? To watch a football game on television?

Jesus was raised in a society in which the Sabbath was strictly kept. A man, for instance, was allowed to walk beside a horse with a hand on the horse's bridle, leading him to a water trough, but was not allowed to carry one end of the rein.

Some of us come from a religious background which was nearly as strict as that one. Church was attended morning and evening. Potatoes for Sunday dinner were peeled the night before. Almost every kind of Sunday activity, with the exception of sleeping and going to church, was frowned on, if not forbidden. Everything else fell under the category of "worldly pleasure." If it gave pleasure (except the heavenly kind, which was not clearly defined), it was wrong to do on Sunday.

Others have come out of a somewhat different religious background. We went to church in the morning, but we could do as we wished the rest of the day. Swimming, professional sports, and picnics —even church picnics—were customary Sunday activities. Sunday evening worship was optional—if it was offered at all.

Still others come out of a secular background, in which Sunday was no different from any other day of the week. Worship was not even considered. Sunday evening was distinctive only because it meant the end of a weekend of working, relaxing, or partying.

What is lawful on Sunday? Is it possible to establish one set of rules for all times, places, and people? It seems that the only way to answer the opening question of this essay is to ask, "What would Jesus do if He were here in person today?" Then, after having answered the question for ourselves, let us not try to impose that answer on others.

INTERPRETIVE COMMENTS

Two incidents recorded in Matthew 12 form the background of this question and point up the difference between the Pharisees and Jesus in their interpretation of correct Sabbath observance.

The first (vv. 1-8) is the dispute in the grain field. The hungry disciples, following Jesus through the field, helped themselves to handfuls of grain. The Pharisees objected, not because the disciples were stealing (the practice was approved by the Old Testament law, Deut. 23:25), but because they were "harvesting" on the Sabbath. This was one of the thirty-nine kinds of activities which were forbidden on the Sabbath.

In response, Jesus did not criticize the old law or contradict its principle—the need for a day of rest. Rather, He pointed out that in certain situations ceremonial law must be superceded by moral law. He cited two significant precedents: the eating of the ceremonial shewbread by David and his men (I Sam. 21:1-6) and the Sabbath day activities of their own priests. The quotation, "I desire mercy, and not sacrifice," is from Hosea 6:6. It makes clear that God intended the holy day to be a blessing rather than a burden.

The second incident (vv. 9-14) took place in the synagogue. Jesus' enemies appear to have known Jesus so well that they anticipated what He was going to do. He answered their question, "Is it lawful to heal on the sabbath?" (v. 10), in two ways: by healing the man's hand, and by asking a question in return (v. 11). Jesus' question about the sheep in the pit points out the absurd self-contradiction in which legalism inevitably entangles itself.

It is ironic that this incident of healing love should trigger the Pharisees' resolve to seek His death (v. 14). How tragic when the form of religion destroys the spirit of it!

DISCUSSION QUESTIONS

1. To what extent does Sunday replace the Old Testament Sabbath? Has there been a change of

meaning? (See Exod. 20:11; Deut. 5:15; Rev. 1:10.) What elements of the Old Testament Sabbath, if any, were meant to be temporary? Does the New Testament give any regulations for keeping the Sabbath? For keeping Sunday? If not, how do we determine what is right and wrong? Or is it no longer a moral issue?

2. How did Jesus approach the question of Sabbath observance? Healing and pulling a sheep out of a pit on the Sabbath are acts of mercy—but can today's recreational activities be included in that category?

3. Consider the additional conflict over the question of plucking grain on the Sabbath (see vv. 1-8 and Mark 2:23-28). How does Jesus' statement, "The sabbath was made for man, not man for the sabbath" (Mark 2:27) cast further light on the subjects of a) Sunday work and b) Sunday recreation?

4. Consider the fact that many people who have strong convictions about Sunday are forced by their employers either to work on Sunday or become liable for loss of wages. In some cases, the employees may even lose their jobs. Does not the practice of Sunday employment discriminate against some people because of their religious preferences?

3

Keeping Traditions

"Why do your disciples transgress the tradition of the elders?" (Matt. 15:2)

Scripture for study: Matthew 15:1-9

Traditions can be very good. The University of Notre Dame, the University of Michigan, Ohio State University, and others have had, for years, a tradition of good football. The observance of Thanksgiving Day has become a venerated American tradition. Some churches have long-standing traditions of strong preaching or generous missionary giving. Certain businesses have traditions of honesty, integrity, and good service. Some cities have established a tradition of justice and equal opportunity for all their citizens. Some people are traditionally cheerful. Most families observe birthdays in some traditional manner. Traditions can be good.

But traditions can be bad as well. Some schools, for instance, have football teams which traditionally lose; some families have a tradition of disharmony; some churches have a tradition of weak religion; and some cities have a tradition of corruption and unequal rights.

Traditions can be bad in other ways. They can form a barrier to progress or lull us into being content with the lesser good. They can even be manipulated, as they were by the Pharisees, into a justification for failure to show compassion and love. A traditionally mission-minded church may fail to see new opportunities on its own doorstep. A student may be content to earn his traditional B when a little extra effort could gain an A. A traditional prayer may never be replaced by a new and vital one.

Why did Jesus and His disciples transgress the traditions of the elders? Because the Savior came with disturbing social pronouncements, radical teachings about personal faith, and startling insights into the nature of God. The religious leaders, trapped in their traditions, were not able to stretch for new truth. The old wineskins could no longer hold the new wine, and the old garment could not cope with the new patch (see Luke 5:36, 37).

INTERPRETIVE COMMENTS

Tradition has always been a major factor in religious practices, but few groups have developed tradition as intricately as had the leaders of Israel. Down through the years, the rabbis had literally added thousands of laws to the laws of Moses.

Hand-washing before meals had originally been required only of priests before they ate sacrifices offered in the Temple (Lev. 22:1-16). Gradually it became imposed upon laymen as well, on all occasions of eating. The scribes even prescribed how much water was to be used and the exact manner in which the handwashing was to be done.

Jesus did not directly answer the criticism. He neither approved the tradition nor condemned it; that was beside the point. They were misusing tradition by making it an end in itself. In the case of the corban practice, they were using a tradition to avoid a moral obligation. *Corban* means "given to God" and refers to a custom of dedicating one's possessions to God. The scribes were apparently using such vows as an excuse for not supporting their aged parents. The scribes may also have been using this method to extract offerings from the people. A devout Jew, in a high peak of religious fervor, might make such a corban vow, then later discover that he was unable to keep that vow and at the same time support his parents. The scribes would insist that at all costs the vow must be kept, even if this meant that the old folks would live in poverty. (Some modern religious groups have used similar tactics to keep the offerings rolling in.) Note that in quoting the commandment regarding honor to parents (vv. 4, 7), Jesus places the moral law above the ceremonial law. Internals rather than externals are the heart of true religion.

DISCUSSION QUESTIONS

1. The radical assumes that most (if not all) tradition is wrong, while the reactionary assumes that most (if not all) tradition is right. So-called liberals, conservatives, and moderates take various positions between these two extreme viewpoints. Where do others see you within this spectrum? Where do you see yourself?

2. Name some cultural traditions of ten, twenty, and fifty years ago which are no longer accepted in your community. Which of these changes are for the better? Which are for the worse? Which have had a mixed effect?

3. Name some of the religious traditions of ten, twenty, and fifty years ago which are no longer accepted as binding in your church. Which of these changes are for the better? Which are for the worse? Which have had a mixed effect?

4. Considering the radical change in traditions during recent years, is it reasonable to assume that similar changes will continue to take place? Which traditions do you think may become obsolete in the near future? Which traditions do you hope will change? Which do you hope will never disappear?

5. Someone has said, "Tradition is the living faith of the dead, while traditionalism is the dead faith of the living." Interpret and evaluate this statement.

4

Helping the Needy

"Where are we to get bread enough in the desert to feed so great a crowd?" (Matt. 15:33).

Scripture for study: Matthew 15:32-39

Jesus had expressed His concern: "I have compassion on the crowd, because they have been with me now three days, and have nothing to eat" (v. 2). But the disciples were skeptical. How can twelve men with very limited resources feed 4,000 people?

Have you ever heard—or said—something like that?

"How can we possibly begin to feed all those starving people in Africa?"

"Sure, minority people ought to have equal opportunities, but we can't change years of tradition in just a few months."

"Yes, I know our municipal court is corrupt, but what can an ordinary citizen like me possibly do about it?"

"We'd like to help with the church building program, but we can't. One can't squeeze blood out of a turnip."

"Yes, I know that jails breed more criminal activity, but there really aren't any better alternatives."

"We know that young people are graduating from our high school without being able to read or write, but we can't keep them here until they are thirty."

These situations do seem almost impossible to remedy—just as it seemed impossible to feed 4,000 hungry people sitting on a hillside in Galilee. Yet on that day, Jesus found a way to feed them all.

Jesus wasn't content to be compassionate, you see. He didn't just voice His concern, then wring His hands, and walk away. He actually did something about it. He seemed to think that if you believe in something strongly enough, you will find a way to get it done.

It's fairly certain that if we are to feed the starving people in Africa we'll have to find an alternative to an on-the-spot miracle; but we can find a way if we really want to. The same goes for teaching the illiterate, helping the alcoholic, rehabilitating the criminal, reviving the ghetto, giving hope to the poverty-stricken, giving freedom to the oppressed, and providing opportunity for those who are the objects of discrimination.

INTERPRETIVE COMMENTS

The reference to Jesus' ministry in Tyre and Sidon (v. 21) and the reference here to how these people "glorified the God of Israel" (v. 31) indicates that this ministry of Jesus may have taken place on the east bank of the Sea of Galilee, which was Gentile territory. A majority of the 4,000 present may have been Gentiles.

The fact that the crowd had stayed with Jesus for three days (v. 32) indicates how intense had been their experience with Christ. Jesus had not only taught them; He had also healed many of the sick, blind, and lame (vv. 30, 31). It was one of those retreats in which all other considerations fade for a time into the background.

Sooner or later, of course, high points of spiritual experience had to concede to necessities of everyday living. The people had to go home to their families, their farms, and their businesses. But there was a more immediate need: the people were hungry. Any food they brought with them had long since been eaten. Jesus and the disciples could not very well say to them, "You've had your spiritual retreat, and that's all you need." Jesus believed that His physical ministry went hand-in-hand with His spiritual ministry.

The loaves were probably barley loaves, and the fish were very likely smoked or pickled—a delicacy often eaten with bread. Notice that the previous feeding of a large crowd (Matt. 14:15-21) began with five loaves and two fishes, while this one begins with seven loaves and a "few" small fish. The previous feeding involved 5,000 people (compared to 4,000 here) and resulted in twelve baskets being left over (compared to seven here).

Some interpreters see in these incidents an extended allegory of the kingdom of God, which is often compared to a great banquet (see Matt. 22:1-14; Luke 14:16-24; 22:30). The five loaves and two fishes represent our human helplessness; Jesus' miracle displays His ability to fill our needs; and the baskets left over represent the overwhelming abundance of God's ultimate provisions. God can do "far more abundantly than all that we ask or think" (Eph. 3:20).

DISCUSSION QUESTIONS

1. It has been suggested by some commentators that this miracle was one of human generosity more than of divine provision. We need not believe, they say, that Jesus actually created food for the 4,000. By pointing out the willingness of the small boy to share his meager fare, He inspired the people to share the lunches they had brought with them. What do you think of the theory that this miracle is one of a human change of attitude? Is there any evidence for it? Is there any evidence to the contrary? What did the Gospel writers believe?

2. Did Jesus provide this food primarily to meet the physical needs of those who were present, or did He do it in order to illustrate a deeper truth about spiritual needs? (See Matt. 16:5-12; John 6:35-71.) Do you think Jesus would have performed the miracle only to provide physical food?

3. Apply the last questions and their answers to a modern mission controversy. Some say Christians should provide food, clothing, and medical care for the have-nots of the world simply because they need these things. Others say that Christian missionaries should provide these services for the purpose of drawing the recipients' attention to Jesus Christ. Do you believe that the first approach is a superficial one, since it ignores people's deep spiritual needs? Do you believe that the second approach is an ignoble one, since it has an ulterior motive in mind?

4. Discuss this miracle in the context of the world hunger problem. What is the real cause of hunger—lack of food or lack of equitable distribution? Does the Marxist system work better than the capitalist system in distributing food? Since it takes

about ten pounds of vegetable food to produce one pound of meat, would the world hunger problem be alleviated if Americans drastically reduced their meat consumption? How can poorer countries be encouraged to become self-reliant in food production? What role can family planning play in the world's food problems?

5

Becoming Great

"Who is the greatest in the kingdom of heaven?" (Matt. 18:1)

Scripture for study: Matthew 18:1-4

Who is the greatest? We all know the world's answer to that question. The greatest is the person who punches the hardest, or looks the sexiest, or is elected chairman, or runs the fastest, or scores the most points, or buys the Rolls Royce, or gets the promotion, or wins the beauty contest, or sells a million records, or writes a best-seller, or moves to the best neighborhood.

In the church, some Christians are considered by others to be spiritually greater because they have been elected elder, or speak in tongues, or contribute 11 percent of their income, or give up a promising career for the kingdom, or attend both morning and evening services. All these are virtues as long as these people stay humble. But as soon as they become selfish and try to gain recognition for doing good works, they are no longer great in God's eyes.

The standard by which Jesus judges greatness is different from those commonly held by both the civil community and the Christian community. The greatest person in Jesus' eyes is "whoever humbles himself like this child" (v. 4).

INTERPRETIVE COMMENTS

According to Mark's account (Mark 9:33, 34), the disciples had been arguing on the way about who was the greatest. They may have been subtle about it, but the effect was the same. Perhaps there was dissension because Peter, James, and John had been selected to go up with Jesus to the mountain where the transfiguration took place (Matt. 17:1-8).

We must "turn," said Jesus (v. 3). The corresponding Hebrew word implies a total repentance. The King James Version says, "Except ye be converted," using a term which implies a comprehensive spiritual change.

When Jesus says that we are to become "like children," (v. 3), He is not implying that children are innocent. We all know that even toddlers can be disobedient, cantankerous, and belligerent.

Nor did he mean that we are to become childish —naive, unschooled, immature. After all, Paul said, "When I became a man, I gave up childish ways" (I Cor. 13:11).

Jesus is referring to certain aspects of childhood related to humility—receptiveness, a willingness to be taught, a sense of wonder, and an honesty of expression. A child is unpretentious, making no effort to seem what he is not. Children tend to be trusting and dependent. They do not make adult distinctions of race, nationality, and social status.

One final observation. It is a sign of the times that we are more apt to ask who is the greatest in the kingdom of earth than we are to ask who is greatest in the kingdom of heaven.

DISCUSSION QUESTIONS

1. Discuss the matter of status within the Christian community. Is the author correct when he implies in the second paragraph that some spiritual endeavors may really be attempts to seem greatest in the kingdom of heaven?

2. Do we sometimes have mixed motives for the religious things we do? Are our real motives sometimes unconscious? Which is more important in God's eyes, the thing we do or the motive behind it? Do you think it is possible to become free of self-seeking motives?

3. Is it ever right to accuse others of doing right things for the wrong reasons? Are there times, for instance, when we have a right to be suspicious about someone who gives a testimony about how much he contributes in the offering or how wonderful it is to speak in tongues? Is it ever possible to judge another person regarding his or her inward motives?

4. What does it mean to humble oneself like a child? What traits was Jesus encouraging? Can these childhood traits be transferred to adult life? What about Paul's words, "When I became a man, I gave up childish ways" (I Cor. 13:11)? Should some characteristics of childhood be retained in adult life? Should others be discarded? Which ones?

6

Forgiving People

"How often shall my brother sin against me, and I forgive him?" (Matt. 18:21).

Scripture for study: Matthew 18:21, 22

It is hard to forgive the brother who got your share of the inheritance, or the friend who stole your doll clothes, or the quarterback who spirited away your girl friend, or the mother-in-law who makes remarks about the person her child could have married, or the neighbor who allows his dog to dig in your flower garden, or the drunk who ran down your daughter.

By most standards, Peter was generous when he offered to forgive a brother seven times. That is four or five more times than I probably would have proposed. After all, you can't let people run all over you. Patience must certainly have its limits. And how can you teach some people to act decently unless you give them the cold shoulder?

But the standards Jesus taught were not like most standards. He advocated such things as walking the second mile, turning the other cheek, and loving your enemy. Somehow, Jesus didn't seem to think that this sort of thing was a sign of sniveling weakness. Rather, He thought of it as a kind of strength —the sort of strength one can have when he has been born anew, when he receives the Spirit of God, when he becomes—by God's power—a new person.

No, the standards Jesus taught weren't like most standards. But neither were the standards by which He lived. He doesn't forgive us just seven times, or 490 times, or even 49,000 times. We can be thankful He practiced what He preached.

INTERPRETIVE COMMENTS

The rabbis taught that three pardons were sufficient, so Peter believed that by doubling that number and adding one more, he was certainly being magnanimous.

When Jesus said, "seventy times seven," He did not mean 490. He means we are to forgive an infinite number of times. More correctly, He meant that we are not to count the number of times we forgive. The person who forgives seven times, for instance, is not really forgiving. That he is keeping count belies a smoldering resentment. And he is really hoping that his antagonist will not change his ways after the seventh offense, because he is planning to nail the scoundrel on the eighth!

But, we ask, are we to forgive someone who does not repent? Even God doesn't do that! He expects us to repent before He forgives us (Mark 1:15; Acts 2:38; 3:19). That is true, but God also took the first step in granting forgiveness. No one begged for a mediator or a sacrifice for sin. "While we were yet sinners Christ died for us" (Rom. 5:8). Our repentance is in response to God's sacrificial love.

Does forgiveness really work? Not always, of

course. Some hardened souls are unresponsive to mercy, preferring to interpret it as weakness. But does nonforgiveness work? Hardly ever. Anger kindles anger, harsh words prompt harsh words, animosity breeds animosity, poison produces poison. In contrast, " A soft answer turns away wrath" (Prov. 15:1), kindness calms the irritated temper, and apology prompts apology. It is more than a coincidence that Saul's Damascus experience (Acts 9:1-9) followed shortly after his garment-holding experience at the stoning of the forgiving Stephen (Acts 7:58–8:1).

The parable of the unforgiving servant which follows (18:23-35) points out that 1) Whatever we have forgiven others is ridiculously small compared to what God has forgiven us, and 2) Our failure to forgive others makes us incapable of receiving God's forgiveness. We pray as Christ taught us, "And forgive us our debts, as we also have forgiven our debtors" (Matt. 6:12).

DISCUSSION QUESTIONS

1. What are some of the things that can happen inwardly to a person when he harbors grudges and nurses resentments? What changes can take place in body chemistry? In physical health? In mental outlook? In personal happiness? In spiritual health? See *None of These Diseases,* by S. I. McMillen (Pillar Books) for excellent resource material on these questions.

2. In the parable of the unforgiving servant (vv. 23-35), what is the ratio of the debt forgiven by the master to the debt not forgiven by the servant? Does the parable imply that we may lose our own

forgiveness if we do not forgive others? What Scripture references support your answer to that question?

3. Is it necessary or even desirable to forgive someone who isn't sorry for what he has done? Does God forgive those who do not repent? What should you do when someone keeps committing the same offense against you, time after time, each time claiming repentance and asking forgiveness?

4. Who should take the first step toward reconciliation, the offending person or the offended person? Who took the initiative to restore the broken relationship between God and man? Discuss how forgiveness can be a powerful force.

7

Guidelines for Divorce

"Is it lawful to divorce one's wife for any cause?" (Matt. 19:3)

Scripture for study: Matthew 19:3-9

Of all of Jesus' teachings on various subjects, this one about marriage must have been one of the most difficult for the males of that day to cope with. Among the accepted reasons for a man to divorce his wife were talking with men, ill-treating her husband's parents, going about with loose hair, and speaking so loudly to her husband that the neighbors could hear. But a wife was permitted to divorce her husband only if he had leprosy. Truly, it was a man's world.

This is also one of the hardest of Jesus' sayings for people to cope with today. There must be some other legitimate grounds for divorce besides adultery, we say; God shouldn't expect two people to continue living together if they are not compatible. Why should a person have to live with a mistake for the rest of his or her life?

In the final analysis, however, the only way to avoid this teaching of Christ is to tear it out of the Bible. If we don't do that, we are stuck with the truth that God designed marriage to be an indissolvable relationship.

Jesus didn't say that marriage is based on sexual compatability, social compatability, similar temperaments, economic prosperity, or personal fulfillment. In fact, he doesn't even say it is based on love. The marriage bond is essentially a bond of *commitment* (v. 5) in which a man and a woman make up their minds that, despite all obstacles, they will make it work. The question is not, "Does he (or she) make me happy?" but "What can I do to make this relationship stable and healthy?"

The problems of a weak marriage are to be solved by working, not by running.

INTERPRETIVE COMMENTS

The question of divorce was already being hotly discussed in Jesus' day. The more conservative rabbis, following the school of Shammai, believed that divorce was permissible only on the grounds of adultery. The more liberal rabbis, following Hillel, allowed a man to divorce his wife on any of many grounds, some of them trivial.

Jesus raised the whole question above the level of a legal pronouncement. He went right to the heart of the matter: God's original plan for marriage. Quoting Genesis 2:24, he pointed out that marriage is designed to be a "one flesh" relationship, implying both intimacy and indissolvability. The "one flesh'" concept probably refers to all levels—physical, psychological, and spiritual—each one enhancing and strengthening the others. This kind of unity made by God cannot properly be dissolved by man.

Note the subtle but significant verb shift in this conversation. The Pharisees said, "Why then did Moses *command* one to give a certificate of divorce?" (v. 7, italics mine), to which Jesus replied, "For your hardness of heart Moses *allowed* you to divorce your wives" (v. 8a, italics mine). How quickly second-best becomes adopted as the norm! How easily permission becomes interpreted as approval! But Jesus stays with the idea: "but from the beginning it was not so" (v. 8b).

DISCUSSION QUESTIONS

1. Some sociologists have pointed out that during the last quarter-century there has been a shift in the basic concept of marriage. Whereas the purpose of marriage was formerly that of giving stability to society, its purpose is now seen as providing personal fulfillment for the participants. Whereas the traditional marriage viewed the man as the head of the home, the modern marriage views the man and woman as equals. Whereas the "glue" that held the traditional marriage together was commitment, the adhesive of the present-day marriage is love.

Do you agree with this analysis? What factors, do you think, have caused the change? What are the strengths of the traditional view of marriage? What are its weaknesses? What are the strengths of the newer view of marriage? What are its weaknesses?

Which kind of marriage is more likely to end in divorce? Which kind is more likely to produce personal satisfaction for both partners? What are the advantages and disadvantages for the children in both kinds? Which type requires the most effort? Is it worth the effort? If you are married, which type do you have? Is it possible to combine the strengths of both?

2. According to Christ's teaching, the only real grounds for divorce is adultery. Does this mean that no other grounds are ever permissible? Since Moses allowed divorce because of human hardness of heart, could we say that Jesus might allow it for the same reason? Is Jesus, in this passage, prescribing an iron-clad rule or is He simply describing the ideal?

3. Is it true that all divorced people who have remarried are continually committing adultery? What if the divorced partner has remarried or died? What if the former mate rejects a proposal to remarry? What if the former mate was the one who committed adultery and insisted on the divorce? What if one of the partners was unfaithful but nevertheless wanted to continue the marriage?

4. Examine the concept of forgiveness as it relates to divorce and remarriage. If we believe that forgiveness removes guilt once and for all, should it not do so when it applies to the sins which break up a marriage?

5. Isn't it true that most divorces could be averted if both partners really wanted to keep the marriage alive? To what extent has the lack of family, society, and church expectation contributed to the divorce rate? To what extent has the legal system contributed to the divorce rate?

6. How should the church treat divorcees? Should it discipline people who are going through or have gone through a divorce? Should the minister and elders try to determine who is the "guilty"

partner? Should a divorced person be permitted to serve on the church governing board? As a Sunday school teacher? As a minister? Should a minister perform a marriage ceremony for a divorcee who is remarrying? Should it be a church wedding?

8

Living Forever

"Teacher, what good deed must I do, to have eternal life?" (Matt. 19:16).

Scripture for study: Matthew 19:16-22

This question and its answer, which are among the most important ones recorded in the Gospels, reveal some important facts about basic needs.

The question shows that there are at least four things that can't give a person peace of mind:

1) Money. The fellow is rich, but he knows money can't buy life.

2) Youth. He is young now, but he knows that the aging process is inevitable.

3) Power. He is a ruler, but such a position is always precarious.

4) Goodness. Even from his earliest years, he has been a decent fellow, but he still has that nagging feeling that things aren't right between himself and a holy God.

Eternal life, says Jesus, will be yours if you do two things: "Go, sell what you possess and give to the poor," and "come, follow me" (v. 21).

Translated into two words, Jesus was saying, repent and believe.

Repentance is the negative change. It is turning away from the false savior (in this case, money). It is realizing that the present course can only lead to hopelessness and despair. It is changing one's mind about ultimate ambitions, priorities, and values.

Belief is the positive change. It is turning toward the true Savior. It is realizing that only Christ has the answer. It is entrusting one's ultimate ambitions, priorities, and values to His leadership. In short, it is "following" Him in this life and into the next.

INTERPRETIVE COMMENTS

This young man certainly seemed sincere. Mark says that he "ran up and knelt before him" (Mark 10:17). He asked the right question, for by asking how to obtain eternal life he went right to the heart of personal religion. We have here the case of a sincere inquirer who failed to enter the kingdom.

Two portions of this narrative are difficult to understand. One has to do with Jesus' apparent rejection of the compliment, "Good Teacher" (Mark 10:17-18). Does this imply that Jesus is denying His own sinlessness? Not necessarily. For one thing, Jesus never made a point of emphasizing His goodness. He didn't flaunt His righteousness even when defending Himself before Pilate. Second, by saying, "No one is good but God alone" (Mark 10:18), Jesus may have been pricking a hole in the young man's balloon. Although Jesus didn't directly challenge the man's claim that He had kept all the commandments from His youth up, He made it clear that any such claim by any human being is presumptuous.

The other difficult portion of the narrative is the apparent claim by Jesus that one can have eternal life by living a good life: "If you would enter life, keep the commandments" (Matt. 19:17). Technically, of course, Jesus is right. A person could earn eternal life if he could obey the law perfectly. But since no one can do this, he must find some other way.

Why was the young man so disappointed? Obviously, he did not want to give up his wealth. That, for him, was too high a price to pay, even for eternal life. We also suspect that he may have been looking for some new command, some innovative approach to spirituality, some radical departure from traditional practice. He may have found that keeping the law from his youth up was a boring and prosaic business. But Jesus could give him no quick formula for sure-fire religion. After giving up your money, He said, you must follow Me. That's a life-long vocation. That implies decades of obedience and servanthood. This, too, was a factor in his sorrowful exodus from the presence of Christ.

DISCUSSION QUESTIONS

1. "Evangelism Explosion" is a program of personal evangelism devised by the Reverend James Kennedy of Coral Ridge Presbyterian Church in Fort Lauderdale, Florida. At the heart of the evangelistic presentation are two questions to be asked of prospective believers:

Have you come to a place in your spiritual life where you can say you know for certain that if you were to die today you would go to heaven?

Suppose that you were to die today and stand before God, and He were to say to you, "Why should I let you into My heaven?" What would you say?

How would you answer these questions?

2. The evangelistic callers in the Kennedy program report that more than 90 percent of the people who respond to the second question say such things as, "I've lived a pretty good life," or "I haven't done many bad things," or "I try to keep the commandments." Do not these answers reflect the basic premise of the rich young ruler, who asked, "What must I *do* to have eternal life?" Is it true that most people, even church members, believe that eternal life is gained by living a good life?

3. The same evangelistic callers report that about 90 percent of the people they call on answer the first question by saying, "I hope so" or "I think so." Are they any more sure about it than the rich young ruler? How much confidence do people really have that their good works will give them eternal life?

4. Discuss Ephesians 2:8-10 in light of the rich young ruler's question.

In verse 8, what is the meaning of grace? What does it mean to have faith? Define gift.

In verse 9, what is included in the word *works*? According to this verse, what is one reason God didn't make salvation contingent on good works? Does this also apply to a person who has taught Sunday school for twenty-seven years and sung in the church choir for nineteen years?

According to verse 10, what is the place of good works in God's plan? Even if our salvation is not built on our good actions, does God intend to see these good things emerge in our lives?

9

Miraculous Power

"How did the fig tree wither at once?" (Matt. 21:20)

Scripture for study: Matthew 21:18-22

Ordinarily, fig trees don't wither in a matter of minutes—or even of hours. Worms, disease, and drought can cause the leaves to crinkle and turn brown, but the process of death creeps slowly over a period of many weeks. This tree died as if it were featured in a time sequence movie—the kind elementary school children see in science class.

The disciples asked how it happened. What *really* caused the tree to wither?

The answer, of course, is divine power. It was divine power that originally caused the fig tree to germinate, grow, photosynthesize, and reproduce. That power would eventually have completed the cycle in death so a new plant could take its place. In this case that divine power had either bypassed or sped up the natural process.

Jesus made an amazing claim. You, too, He said to His disciples, have access to miraculous energy. You, too, can be conduits of divine power. You, too, can perform miracles.

There is only one requirement: you must have faith. You must believe it can be done. You must trust completely in the Source. You must believe in the impossible. Then you can say to a mountain, "Be taken up and cast into the sea" and it will be done (v. 21).

There is no record that the disciples actually ever did anything quite like that. Jesus never meant for His followers to capriciously move mountains around. (Can you imagine the problems this would cause with the Environmental Protection Agency?) Nevertheless, we keep hearing examples of mountains that people move when they, by faith, unleash divine power.

By faith, a mountain of seemingly overwhelming tasks can be cut down to a small hill that is possible to climb.

By faith, we can remove mountains of anger, despair, defeat, discouragement, loneliness, and weakness.

By faith, the cool wind of love can be invited to swirl around the mountains of marital disharmony, filling in the deep gullies of silence and resentment.

By faith, the wind of the Spirit can be unleashed on the mountain of destructive addictions, destroying the desire in a matter of hours.

By faith, the mountain of sin which blocks the way to heaven can be washed away in a windstorm of forgiveness, never to be seen again.

INTERPRETIVE COMMENTS

Some commentators have made an interesting observation regarding the fig tree, namely, that Jesus cursed the tree not because it had no figs, but because it was false. As Mark records, it was not the season for figs (Mark 11:13), so Jesus had no reason to expect the tree to have fruit. But the tree did have leaves. This was strange, since the fruit ordinarily precedes the leaves. Thus the tree, by displaying leaves, was pretending to have fruit, to be something it was not.

Was Jesus using the fig tree as an illustration of the people of Israel—pretending to be religious, but not producing the appropriate fruit? That's the imagery in a parable He used, as recorded in Luke 13:6-9. It's possible that this is the lesson Jesus was intending to teach, but that the disciples' question about the power that performed the miracle led Jesus off into a different homily.

DISCUSSION QUESTIONS

1. What is a miracle? Is it an act that bypasses the natural process? Can a miracle be such mostly because of its timing, such as the parting of the Red Sea (caused by the blowing of a strong wind all night)? Does a miracle contradict natural law? Or is it simply a higher form of natural law which we are not acquainted with and are unable to understand in this life?

2. Do you believe some people today have God-given power to perform miracles? Does the possession of such a gift mean that one is a more "spiritual" Christian than others? What about non-Christians who have a reputation for being able to perform miracles of healing or other kinds of extraordinary feats? How do you account for their abilities, if indeed they are real? Can an analogy

be made to the Christian's use of talents as over against a non-Christian's use of talents?

3. How literal was Jesus intending to be when He said that His disciples would be able to move mountains if they had faith? Is a changed life as much a miracle as a changed fig tree or a moved mountain?

4. Has a miracle ever taken place in the life of a friend or relative? Has a miracle ever taken place in your own life? Was it primarily physical? Spiritual? Moral? Personal?

10

Obeying the Government

"Is it lawful to pay taxes to Caesar, or not?"
(Matt. 22:17)

Scripture for study: Matthew 22:15-22

It was meant to be a trick question, designed so that either a yes or no answer would get Jesus into trouble.

Jesus didn't oblige His critics by answering yes or no. He said, "Render therefore to Caesar the things that are Caesar's, and to God the things that are God's (v. 21).

Was Jesus simply avoiding their trap? Was He being wishy-washy in order to keep out of trouble? No, I think not. Jesus never distinguished Himself by using excessive diplomacy.

He was pointing out some very important principles about the Christian's relationship to his government, whatever kind of government it may be.

1) Seldom can these questions be answered with a simple yes or no. There is much more involved than simply being "lawful" or "unlawful." Consider, for instance, the civil rights marches in the United States which disobeyed local parade regulations,

and the evangelistic efforts in communist countries which disobey government regulations.

2) God's people must take seriously their responsibilities toward their government, no matter what form of government it is. Rome's government was dictatorial, pagan, and imperialistic; yet Jesus (in this case) urged neither active nor passive resistance.

3) Christians must take even more seriously their responsibilities to God. Their relationship to the heavenly Lord is even more important than their relationship to their earthly lords. Sometimes the two responsibilities will coincide and sometimes they will conflict, depending on the time, place, persons, and circumstances.

INTERPRETIVE COMMENTS

A common enemy can produce strange allies! The Pharisees were conservatives, loyal to the cause of Jewish independence. The Herodians were liberals, advocates of loyalty to King Herod Antipas. But they decided to become buddies for a time and make a call on Jesus. Obviously, no matter how Jesus answered their question, He would offend one side or the other.

The tax alluded to was probably the much-resented poll tax, levied on all those under Roman rule. The coin, a denarius, probably bore the likeness of either Tiberius or Augustus, with appropriate inscriptions.

Most commentators agree that Jesus did, indeed, advocate that the tax be paid. Caesar's inscription on the coin was symbolic not only of his authority but also of the benefits of his rule—an atmosphere of security in which trade could be carried on, a highway system paid for by taxes, a stable government, and police protection against theft and bodily harm. Although one of Jesus' disciples (Simon the Zealot) was a radical right-winger, Jesus had no sympathy with radical nationalism. He had on another occasion (John 6:15) resisted the efforts of the people to make Him their king, which would have placed Him in the role of a revolutionary.

The Christians of the first century faithfully imitated Jesus' nonrevolutionary attitude toward the government, but they got into trouble with the Caesars anyway. Ironically, their persecution was triggered by their obedience to Jesus' second precept, "Render . . . to God the things that are God's" (v. 21). They paid Caesar both taxes and honor, but when it came to worship, they drew the line. Even patriotism has its limits, and for adhering to these limits they paid with their lives.

DISCUSSION QUESTIONS

1. Should the Christian church in communist countries try to peacefully coexist with the government? Are the cooperative pastors compromising their faith? Are the dissident pastors harming the cause of Christ by inciting harsher repression? Is Bible smuggling right or wrong?

2. Is it right to pay taxes to the government, knowing that a large portion will be spent on the military? What about the pacifists who deduct this portion from their tax bill and give it to benevolent causes?

3. Is it right to participate in an illegal demonstration? Which of the following do you believe

have the right to demonstrate: a) supporters of the Equal Rights Amendment, b) antiabortion groups, c) gay activists, d) the Ku Klux Klan, e) civil rights activists, f) communists, g) supporters of Bible reading and prayer in schools? How much is your answer influenced by the particular cause promoted?

4. Is it ever right to refuse to testify in a court of law? Under what kind of circumstance can we disobey this civil authority?

5. What are some of the things we ought to "render to Caesar"? What are some of the things we ought to "render to God"?

6. What further light does Romans 13:1-7 cast on this subject? In view of these teachings of Paul, was the American Revolution justified?

11

The Most Important
Commandment

"Teacher, which is the great commandment?"
(Matt. 22:35)

Scripture for study: Matthew 22:34-40

Maybe I'm too suspicious, but I get the feeling
that the questioner was really trying to find out
which commandments are the least important, so
he would know which could be broken with less
fear of punishment.

It was meant to be a trick question, designed so
that either a yes or no answer would get Jesus into
a cop-out; he got an answer that challenged him to
reach for the ultimate.

The greatest commandment, said Jesus, is love.
In so saying He raised Christianity's ethical ideal to
the highest possible level while at the same time
neither destroying nor contradicting Judaism's law.

The greatest commandment is a *summary* of the
Ten Commandments. The first four commandments
simply explain in greater detail how we can love
God; and the last six commandments show spe-
cifically how we can love others. Refusing to steal,
for instance, is just one way of loving another
person.

The greatest commandment also reveals the *spirit* of the Ten Commandments. Jesus is saying that it isn't enough for us to do the right thing; we must do the right thing for the right reason. We should refrain from stealing, for instance, not just because we are afraid of getting caught, but because we love other people and God.

The greatest commandment is also the *supreme expression* of the Ten Commandments. The Ten Commandments reveal the minimum; the great commandment reveals the maximum. The Ten Commandments say, "You shall not," while the great commandment says, "You shall." The Ten Commandments direct us to avoid evil, while the great commandment tells us to seek good. It's not enough, for instance, not to steal from others; we must actively promote their good.

INTERPRETIVE COMMENTS

Jesus' "new" commandment was not really new. Every pious Jew recited the *Shema,* Deuteronomy 6:5, every day. With this exhortation to love God, Jesus combined Leviticus 19:18, a command to love one's neighbor as oneself. Thus, in one beautiful sentence Jesus summarized the many hundreds of Old Testament laws.

Jesus added the words, "On these two commandments depend all the law and the prophets" (v. 40) to point out that His great commandment sums up more than the Pentateuch, the first five books of the Bible; it epitomizes the prophets as well. This is significant, because the prophetic writings were in a sense a fuller and more advanced revelation than were the Books of the Law. In general, the prophets emphasized the life of the inner being, the motives of the heart, more than did Moses (although both parts of Jesus' quote are from the writings of Moses!).

By placing first the principle of loving God, Jesus implies that our relationship with the Father is the primary, the all-pervading relationship of life. On it all other relationships are based. If we love God, we will be more inclined to love other people, who are created in the image of God.

Even our love for God has an antecedent: "We love him, because he first loved us" (I John 4:19, KJV). These commandments are intimately inter-woven with the entire New Testament message of good news through Jesus Christ.

The Greek word used here is not *eros,* romantic love, or *philia,* friendly love. The word is *agape,* self-giving, deep, sacrificing love. It is a love which finds its strength, not in the attractiveness of the object loved, but in the will of the person who loves.

DISCUSSION QUESTIONS

1. What would be the disadvantages of having the Ten Commandments only, without the love commandment? What would be the disadvantage of having the love commandment only, without the Ten Commandments? What unique contribution does each make to the moral code?

2. Is it possible to be in a situation which compels us to disobey one of these commandments in order to keep the other? In *Holocaust,* for instance, Carl's German wife Inga permits a warden of the prison camp to have sex with her in exchange for permitting her to deliver letters to her imprisoned

husband. Other chronicles of World War II relate stories of mothers who did the same in order to secure food for their children. If a decision must be made between one of the Ten Commandments and the love commandment, which should we choose? Are we guilty, then, of disobeying the other?

3. Which of the Ten Commandments do you believe are disobeyed by the largest number of people today? Which are no longer considered relevant by great segments of the population? Which are still highly regarded? Do any of them seem out of date because of the passing of years and the changing of society?

12

The Second Coming

*"What will be the sign of your coming and
of the close of the age?" (Matt. 24:3)*

Scripture for study: Matthew 24:3-8, 36-39

During the last decade Christians have shown an
extraordinary interest in the second coming of
Christ. Hundreds of authors have felt moved to
write books on the subject, most espousing the one
true interpretation of biblical prophecy. Preachers
and evangelists take note of earthquakes, famines,
uprisings, Mideast problems, and disasters of all
kinds; then go to the Bible to find references to
these events. In short, they are trying to answer for
themselves the question the disciples asked Jesus:
"When will this be, and what will be the sign of
your coming and of the close of the age?"

Jesus took a different view of these matters than
do most modern interpreters of prophecy. As for
the calamities, implies Jesus, don't get too excited
about them; they will always be common occur-
rences on the earth (vv. 6-8). As for the self-
appointed messiahs, reject them (vv. 4, 5). As for
those who predict that the end is near, ignore them,

for God hasn't revealed that information to anyone (v. 36).

As a matter of fact, says Jesus, the last days will be deceptively normal. They will be "as were the days of Noah," with people eating, drinking, and marrying (vv. 37, 38). There is really nothing so unusual about that.

The point is that the end will come without warning. It will be a surprise to those who have ignored it and to those who have made a science of predicting it.

The only thing that really matters is to be like Noah—prepared.

INTERPRETIVE COMMENTS

In this passage Jesus is more concerned about warning His followers about being duped and panicked by false teachers than He is about giving a precise blueprint for the future.

Beware, said Jesus, of false messiahs (v. 5). Three would-be saviors are already mentioned in the Book of Acts (5:36, 37; 21:38). Many religious movements today feed on the ego of their leaders, who claim new revelations from God and are extraordinarily adept at raising money.

Verses 6-9 mention four types of calamities: 1) wars and rumors of wars, 2) famines, 3) earthquakes, and 4) persecution of Christians. These horrors are usually interpreted as signs of the end. It would seem to me, however, that Jesus is saying just the opposite: "See that you are not alarmed; for this must take place, but the end is not yet" (v. 6). He is saying, in effect, "These upheavals are going to be common on earth during every generation, so don't let some fanatic stampede you into thinking that the end is near." And so it has been. With each new earthquake, famine, war, or wave of persecution there has been a new outbreak of end-time prophecy—but no outbreak of the end time. The danger of this sort of thing is best illustrated by the well-known story of the shepherd boy who cried "Wolf!"

DISCUSSION QUESTIONS

1. How accurate were most of the prophecy books which flooded the Christian bookstores in the early to mid-70s? The class members may wish to arrive at an answer by each giving a report on a certain prophecy book which was published two or more years ago. Include in the reports such items as a) specific events which the author believes are fulfillments of prophecy, b) signs which indicate to the author that the end is near, c) the author's predictions about things to come, d) the author's emphasis on various calamities, and e) the projected date of the second coming (or at least the rapture of the saints).

2. Simultaneous with a renewed Christian interest in biblical prophecy, there has been a revival of interest in astrological and psychic prophecy on the other side of the spectrum—by people who have little or no Christian beliefs. Discuss the possible reasons for this.

3. Do you believe that a preoccupation with the second coming of Christ and with the end of the age is a good thing? What are the positive benefits of believing that the end is near? What are the negative effects? Discuss the previous questions as they relate to a) evangelism, b) social action programs, and c) the credibility of the gospel.

13

Loyalty

"Is it I, Lord?" (Matt. 26:22)

Scripture for study: Matthew 26:20-25

Is it I, Lord, who betrayed You?

Did I betray You when I bargained with the chief priests for thirty pieces of silver? Or had I already betrayed You when I objected to the tearful attention being given Your feet by that weeping woman?

Is it I, Lord, who betrayed You?

Did I betray You when I dragged Your name through the gutter at the cocktail party? Did I betray You when I put two dollars in the offering plate after spending twenty-two dollars the night before at a restaurant?

When was it, Lord, that I betrayed You?

Was it when I referred to some of Your people as dagos, or niggers, or kikes? Or was it when I pretended to know nothing about those payoffs at the city council? Or was it when I made those suggestive, off-color remarks at the office?

Perhaps it was that time a few months ago when I disillusioned my children. Or when I substituted shoddy material because it would be covered up anyway and would not be apparent for a few years. Or maybe it was the time I said, "Let them starve. It'll help take care of the population explosion over there."

Is it I, Lord, who am betraying You?

Is it I who am harboring a smoldering grudge against a brother? Is it I who am spreading rumors about one of Your local and effective—but imperfect —servants? Is it I who am committing those sins which only You and I know about?

Is it I, Lord, who am betraying You?

INTERPRETIVE COMMENTS

Eating together, for the people of Jesus' day, meant love and loyalty. Even a common meal symbolized mutual trust, for it barred any hostile acts between the participants. This, together with the fact that the Twelve had been companions together with Jesus for three years, intensified the shock of Jesus' disclosure.

We cannot be sure what each disciple meant when he asked, "Lord, is it I?" It may be that each was sincerely asking the question; it may also be that each was using the question to exonerate himself in the eyes of the others.

The dish to which Jesus referred (v. 23) may have been the *haroseth* sauce into which the bitter herbs were dipped. At any meal, all those present dipped into one common dish. Jesus' statement emphasized the insidious nature of the betrayal rather than narrowing down the "suspects."

"The Son of man goes" (v. 24) no doubt refers to His going to His death. The juxtaposition of "as it is written of him" and "woe to that man by whom the Son of man is betrayed" is an interesting commentary on determinism and free will. Jesus affirmed both doctrines. On one hand He stated that His death was predicted by Scripture and therefore inevitable; yet on the other hand He stated that the betrayer is fully responsible for his part in that event.

DISCUSSION QUESTIONS

1. When Jesus chose His disciples, did He know that Judas would betray Him? If so, why did He pick one so obviously unqualified? If Jesus didn't know, does this imply that His foreknowledge was severely limited?

2. What, do you think, motivated Judas to betray Jesus? Suggest some of the theories you have heard. Is it possible, as some suggest, that Judas had a good motive, but that his plans went awry? Did Jesus consider him to be guilty or innocent?

3. Is it too harsh to imply that dragging Jesus' name through the gutter at a cocktail party (see essay) is betraying Jesus? Would it be more accurate to say that this is denying Him rather than betraying Him? What is the difference between the two? How are the two offenses similar?

4. Are the offenses listed in the essay more serious when committed by a Christian than when committed by a non-Christian? What responsibility does the believer have that the unbeliever does not have?

14

Choosing Friends

"Why do you eat and drink with tax collectors and sinners?" (Luke 5:30)

Scripture for study: Luke 5:29-32

Let's phrase the question a bit differently: "Why do you hang around with that crowd? Why do you keep that kind of company?"

If you were to ask that question of a number of people, you might receive such answers as:

"We've got a lot in common."

"They accept me as one of them."

"Who likes to drink alone?"

"We have some really wild times."

"They are my kind of people."

Hanging around with "publicans and sinners," you see, is not in itself a virtue. It may simply verify an old adage that "birds of a feather flock together."

With Jesus, it was different. He was a bird of quite a different feather. He did not share these people's rebelliousness, dishonesty, irreligion, and national disloyalty. He did not need their friendship in order to alleviate His loneliness or to give Him a feeling of acceptance and worth.

Why, then, did Jesus eat and drink with that rowdy crowd? *Because He had something to share with them.* His friendship. His love. His views of life and death. His insights about God, forgiveness, and heaven. His acceptance of them as people of eternal worth. He came, He said, as a physician (v. 31).

A physician always takes a risk of contacting the disease from the patient. Therefore we must double check both our motives and our immunity when befriending non-Christians.

INTERPRETIVE COMMENTS

Not only did Jesus eat with publicans; He called one of them to be a disciple. To Levi, the tax collector (called Matthew in the first Gospel), He said, "Follow me." It is sensible to assume that Levi had had some previous contact with Christ. Perhaps the tax collector had talked with Jesus on a few occasions, or perhaps Jesus had spotted him hanging around at the edge of the crowd for many days, listening intently to what He had to say. Whatever the circumstance, we may be sure that the invitation was neither given nor accepted lightly. It was no small thing for Levi to do, because in following Jesus he left a well-paying job.

Levi did not leave his old friends, however. He didn't say, "Now that I've found something better, I don't need you." Instead he began immediately to integrate the old and the new in his life by inviting his old friends and his new Master to the same dinner party. Jesus' spirit of acceptance was genuine, so no one felt awkward or out of place.

When Jesus said, "I have not come to call the

righteous, but sinners to repentance," He did not imply that the Pharisees were righteous. Rather, He meant that those who acknowledge themselves as sinners will find in Him their forgiveness and salvation, while those who imagine themselves to be righteous will ignore His invitation as if it does not apply to them.

DISCUSSION QUESTIONS

1. Doesn't it seem opportunistic to befriend people for the purpose of saving their souls? Isn't it manipulative when we try to get people's confidence for the sake of winning them over to our point of view? On the other hand, isn't telling someone about Christ the best evidence of really caring? Can we truly be a friend without sharing the best news of all? How did Jesus manage to be a true "physician" through personal friendship, without being manipulative?

2. How much do your friends influence you in the way you think and act? In what ways is this influence obvious and overt? In what ways is it subtle? What has more impact on you, the influence of personal friends or the influence of society in general? Do these two factors influence us in different ways?

3. Why do most alcohol and other drug rehabilitation centers insist that the first step in a cure is to remove the person from his environment? What do you think of the statement, "He was a good boy, but he got in with the wrong crowd"? Don't people—including young people—usually pick friends whose values are similar to their own?

4. What are the advantages of having non-Christian friends? What are the disadvantages? Do Christians necessarily have better morals and values than non-Christians? Should we ever refuse to be a friend of someone because of his or her religion —or lack of it?

15

Defending Jesus

"Lord, do you want us to bid fire come down from heaven and consume them?" (Luke 9:54)

Scripture for study: Luke 9:51-56

There are always some people who, like James and John, are ready to defend Jesus with fire. In fact, they go one step farther than those two "sons of thunder." Instead of being content to call down God's fire from heaven, they feel it necessary to build their own. Some of the saddest chapters of Christian history are about burnings at the stake, boilings in oil, stretchings on the rack, dank imprisonments, and torture with spiked boots—all in the name of the good news of Jesus Christ.

Unfortunately, that day is still not past. Crosses are still burned and bombs are still ignited by those who believe they are called by God to encourage blacks, Jews, and other minorities to "know their place." Mimeographs still crank out Scripture-quoting hate sheets. Whisper campaigns are conducted against pastors who don't say the right words. In almost every denomination a few feel an obligation to oppose every policy and proposal of their denominational executives. Modern sons and daughters of thunder still stand up at congregational meetings and wax eloquent in "holy" rage.

In answer to the question of James and John, Jesus responded with a rebuke. To those who, in these enlightened days, are still building fires in the name of Christ—without bothering to ask His permission—the Prince of Peace must be responding with frustration and sorrow.

INTERPRETIVE COMMENTS

With this verse (v. 51) the author begins narrating a new era in Jesus' life. Previously Jesus had spent most of His time at home base, Galilee. His ministry there reached a climax with Peter's great confession (v. 20) and with the transfiguration on the mountain (vv. 28-36). Then he "set his face to go to Jerusalem" (v. 51), a trip that would ultimately lead to the cross. Luke devotes the next ten chapters to recording Jesus' actions and teachings on that journey.

Unlike most Jewish travelers, Jesus went through the center of Samaria rather than going around it. He found—as could be expected—a cold response. Galilean prophets were not at the top of local popularity polls in Samaria. The Samaritans would not so much as "receive him"—allow Him to eat and sleep at their inns.

One can be somewhat sympathetic with James and John. They were "high" on Jesus. They had seen His glory, caught a glimpse of eternity, and heard the Father's word of approval. How could the Samaritans be so blind? Why couldn't everyone recognize Christ for who He was?

It would seem that their reactions were based on three things: 1) their culturally-induced dislike for the Samaritans, 2) their zeal for Christ, and 3) their own explosive personalities (in Mark 3:17 they are nicknamed "sons of thunder"). It is sometimes difficult to distinguish between our cultural prejudices and our religious convictions.

DISCUSSION QUESTIONS

1. Name some ways in which the cause of Christ is defended in a questionable way today. Do the ends ever justify the means?

2. Analyze some literature published by Christian groups which attacks the position of other Christian groups. Does this literature stick to the issues, or does it attack personalities? Does it use inflammatory language? Does it document its charges? Does it allow for differences of opinion within the Christian community? Does it address other believers as brothers and sisters in Christ?

3. Do you believe Madalyn Murray O'Hair has been treated in an honorable way by Christians and the Christian press? Do you think that if she ever becomes a believer, it will be because of the fine examples of Christian love displayed to her by the Christian community? How should we deal with her and with others who have publically opposed the Christian gospel and the Christian church?

4. Jesus received the same kind of treatment at the hands of the Samaritans as blacks used to receive in America, especially in the south—refusal of food or lodging. The disciples advocated violence in setting right this wrong, but Jesus quelled their

enthusiasm. Can we draw legitimate analogies to Jesus' experience to modern-day civil rights matters? What methods of bringing about justice do we have to choose from? What method did Jesus choose?

16

Choosing Neighbors

"And who is my neighbor?" (Luke 10:29)

Scripture for study: Luke 10:29-37

Who are my neighbors?

Certainly not the children of China. Let the communists take care of their own.

Certainly not the people of India. They'd have a lot more food if they would kill a few of those sacred cows.

Who are my neighbors?

Certainly not that young couple living in the apartment down the hall. They aren't married. To be friendly would be to condone that sort of thing.

Certainly not the blacks in the ghetto. We paid a lot of money to get into a school district far away from them.

Certainly not the people across the street. The husband comes home drunk at 2 o'clock almost every morning, and you'd think his wife would know enough to stop having kids. And I've heard their son is gay.

Certainly not the members of the motorcycle gang who hang around the gas station. The skulls and crossbones embroidered on their black leather jackets show what kind of people they are.

Who is my neighbor?

Certainly not that pregnant high school sophomore. Our daughter shouldn't be associating with a girl who has that kind of reputation.

Certainly not that weirdo in my class. Once I say a kind word to him, he'll stick with me like a leech.

Certainly not that crotchety old Mrs. Winslow. If she really is lonely, as she claims, she shouldn't complain so much. Who wants to listen to that?

Who is my neighbor?

Certainly not that man lying there beside the road. How do I know it isn't some sort of trick? Besides, I'm already late for church. . . ."

INTERPRETIVE COMMENTS

Interestingly enough, this young lawyer asked Jesus the same question the rich young ruler asked Him (Luke 18:18-23). Apparently the question was brewing in the hearts of many.

The young man showed extraordinary insight into the essence of the law (v. 27), but apparently was not yet willing to put it fully into practice (v. 29).

The parable of the good Samaritan is perhaps more than a parable. It may have been based on an actual happening the hearers were acquainted with. At the least, its locale was the actual road between Jericho and Jerusalem.

When Jesus said that the man was going "down" from Jerusalem, he meant it. That road drops more than thirty-four hundred feet in less than seventeen miles. The Jewish historian Josephus called it "desolate and rocky." In the fourth century Jerome called it "the bloody way" and said that it was still in-fested with robbers.

Since many thousands of priests lived in Jericho, and since all religious functions were performed at the Temple in Jerusalem, the priests and the Levites were probably on their way to or from their sacred duties. In a sense, the wounded man was one of their parishioners. But it took a layman—one of the wrong religion and nationality besides—to per-form a truly spiritual act on the Jericho road.

Oil and wine were widely used for medicinal purposes in that day. Two denarii would have been enough for several day's lodging, and the Samaritan was prepared to pay more if necessary.

DISCUSSION QUESTIONS

1. Being a "good Samaritan" often involves tak-ing a risk. A person who tries to interfere with a mugging, for instance, is likely to get hurt. What are some other situations in which a would-be helper might get hurt, killed, or sued?

2. Risks can also be psychological. People who take care of foster children, for instance, may de-velop loving attachments, only to have them broken traumatically when the children are sent back to their natural parents or relatives. What are some other situations in which those who become good neighbors make themselves vulnerable for deep hurts?

3. Is there a certain group, class, nationality, or race which you find difficult to accept as "neigh-bors"? What has caused you to feel the way you do? Do you suppose the Samaritan in the parable had similar negative feelings toward Jews?

4. How can you overcome a long-standing prejudice? If, for instance, your religious upbringing has taught you to dislike Roman Catholics, how can you overcome it? If your family has taught you to think negatively about Jews, how do you throw off that family influence?

5. It has been suggested that the good Samaritan, after he returned home, should have gone one step farther: he should have tried to lobby for better police protection for the Jericho road. In other words, it isn't always enough to treat the symptoms of a disease; we also have to try to find a way to cure it and prevent it. What do you think? How can we apply this same kind of thinking to the problem of world hunger? Troubled marriages? Crime? Child abuse?

17

Evangelistic Prospects

"Then who can be saved?" (Luke 18:26)

Scripture for study: Luke 18:26

Nearly all churches have a "prospect list" (although they may refer to it with a more religious-sounding term)—that includes people who have signed the visitors' cards, recently moved into the community, or been suggested by members of the church.

The minister may place these names on cards, then file the cards in such a way that the most promising prospects are in front. If he or his evangelistic callers make visits, they will use the front cards first. Then, if they have time, they will call on the others.

What determines a "promising prospect"? The most obvious factors are evidence of receptivity to the gospel, an openness to spiritual things, a spirit of inquiry—and yes, sometimes social status and wealth. The names at the bottom of the list are likely to be those who have seemed hostile, unfriendly, or indifferent.

You can't blame preachers for using that kind of

rating system. Their time is limited, and there is some truth in that old saying that you shouldn't waste your time tugging on green fruit.

Nevertheless, the conversation with the ruler haunts us. Here was a man whose name would be on the top card of any caller's prospect list. He was young, bright, religiously-inclined, inquisitive about eternal life—and yes, rich. But he turned out to be one of the poorest prospects Jesus ever talked to. The very things we thought were pluses turned out to be minuses. The young man walked sadly away, still an unbeliever.

In the next chapter we meet a man whose name should be at the bottom of the pile of prospect cards. He is socially maladjusted, antireligious, dishonest, and physically unappealing. His name is Zacchaeus.

Maybe we ought to reshuffle our cards.

INTERPRETIVE COMMENTS

Jesus' statement about a camel going through the eye of a needle (v. 25) is one of His witty analogies, similar in nature to that of the blind man leading a blind man (Matt. 15:14). It proves, for one thing, that Jesus had a sense of humor. It also dramatically makes the point that wealth may be a serious impediment to salvation.

Such a statement must have been shocking to the Jews, who generally believed that wealth was a sign of God's favor. It was widely taught that God rewards His good people with riches, and punishes bad people with poverty. Thus the onlookers' question, "Then who can be saved?" (v. 20) means, "If even the rich people hardly have a chance, what about us ordinary folks?" Jesus replies that all things are possible with God. It takes a miracle to save rich and poor alike, and God is up to both.

DISCUSSION QUESTIONS

1. Why would Jesus say such a thing as, "How hard it is for those who have riches to enter the kingdom of God!"? (v. 24). Does this imply that there is something inherently deficient in the character of the rich? What requirements of true religion might rich people find difficult to accept?

2. Is it true that churches sometimes choose to call first on the appealing, well-to-do couples of the neighborhood, and only afterwards on the poorer and less socially acceptable? Is there even an unspoken hope that "certain kinds" of people will not choose to come to this church?

3. Someone has said that "Getting Ahead" is America's most popular religion. People work their way up the corporate ladder with religious fervor; children are "sacrificed" by neglect; and people display their "idols'" on water, land, and air with religious intensity. Is this a fair analysis? Can striving for success indeed become a substitute religion, involving sacrifices, gods, and rituals of all kinds?

4. Why do some people who seem religiously-inclined turn down the gospel? Why do some who seem antagonistic eventually accept it? Is there any way of predicting who is "ready" for Christian faith and who is not?

18

Life in Heaven

"In the resurrection, therefore, whose wife will the woman be?" (Luke 20:33)

Scripture for study: Luke 20:27-40

Disregard the fact that this question about the resurrection was asked by people who didn't believe in the resurrection.

Disregard, also, the opinion expressed by some present-day wags that Jesus' answer (v. 35) is one of the greatest promises in the Bible.

Instead, observe the great truth implied here: heaven's relationships and heaven's pleasures will be quite unlike those on earth.

It is hard to imagine life without romantic love. We are prisoners of our own space and time. We are limited by our own experiences and values. It is difficult to imagine what life would be like in a new dimension, and it is almost impossible to comprehend the freedom we will experience when we no longer are confined by the limitations of our physical bodies.

How would you describe to an unborn child what life is like outside the warm, dark place in which he now floats? How would you tell that fetus about dandelions and tigers and fluffy clouds and teddy bears and Disneyland and airplanes and sex and Beethoven?

You can't, of course; and neither is it possible for God to explain exactly what heaven will be like.

We can be certain, however, that singing in the spirit will be far more melodious than singing in the flesh, and that love in the spirit will make love in the flesh seem shoddy indeed. Marriage is part of God's love-design for us here, and it is well-adapted to our needs on this small planet. But we can be sure that He has a grander love-design for life in heaven, well-adapted to the infinite possibilities of that existence.

INTERPRETIVE COMMENTS

This question was asked by the Sadducees, the "liberals" of the day, in hopes of discrediting both the doctrine of the resurrection and Jesus Himself.

It now seems strange to us, but the Mosaic law (Deut. 25:5-10) directed that if a man dies and leaves no child, one of his brothers shall marry the widow. The first-born son of that union will take the name of the deceased, thus perpetuating the family name and the family inheritance. Jesus' answer to the question about this law avoids the trap of contradicting the Mosaic law while at the same time affirming the doctrine of the resurrection. Not only that, it gives a somewhat startling new revelation about life in heaven.

God has created our minds and bodies to be well-adapted to life on earth. Earth has oxygen, so we have lungs to breathe it. Earth has sunlight, so we have eyes that are sensitive to its rays. If the entire earth had been covered with water we may have had gills instead of lungs; and if the earth had always been in darkness we may have been born with sonar equipment instead of eyes.

Life on this planet always ends in death, so if the race is to survive there has to be a plan for propagation. God has beautifully designed that plan.

Life on this planet can also be harsh, lonely, and brutal. If we are to survive there must also be love, companionship, comfort, and pleasure. God also has beautifully designed those amenities into His plan.

Heaven will not be like earth, for old things will have passed away and all things will have become new. It will be a new mode of reality, a new dimension, an existence without parallel here. The Bible tells us there will be no sunlight there (Rev. 21:23), so we won't need eyes as we now have them. If there is no oxygen there, we won't need lungs. If there is no death there, we won't need to be equipped for reproduction. If life won't be lonely and harsh, we won't need the kind of companionship we need now.

We don't know exactly what heaven will be like, but we can be sure that heaven's light will make earth's light look dim.

DISCUSSION QUESTIONS

1. Even if we won't be married in heaven, in the earthly sense, do you think we will be able to recognize each other? What clues can we get from Jesus' postresurrection appearances? After the resur-

rection, in what ways was Jesus similar to the way He had been before? How was He different?

2. What insights does I Cor. 15:35-50 give to the subject of life on earth versus life in heaven?

3. Did the Greeks of Jesus' day believe in immortality of the soul? Did they find it easy to believe in the resurrection of the dead (see Acts 17:31, 32)? Which is emphasized more in the New Testament—the immortality of the soul or the resurrection of the dead? Which doctrine seems to receive more emphasis today? For a good discussion of this subject, see Oscar Cullmann's *Immortality of the Soul or Resurrection of the Dead* (Allenson, 1958).

4. Are the biblical pictures of heaven meant to be literal or figurative? Will the streets, for instance, be made of earth-style gold, and will the gates be made of earth-style pearls? (see Rev. 21:10-21). If not, what meaning do the biblical descriptions convey?

5. Read *Life After Life*, by Raymond A. Moody, Jr., (Bantam, 1976) or some other book which relates the experiences of people who have been technically dead or nearly dead, but lived to tell about the experience. How do these experiences substantiate biblical teaching about the life to come? At what point do these experiences seem to differ from biblical teachings? Do these experiences relate a full-fledged heaven or do they describe the very earliest stages of the hereafter?

19

Believing in Jesus' Deity

"Are you the Son of God?" (Luke 22:70)

Scripture for study: Luke 22:66-71

Sometimes what you think of a certain person isn't really that important to you. The girl at the checkout counter who overcharged you a dime—did she make a mistake or did she do it intentionally? As long as you get your dime back, you don't really care.

At other times your evaluation of another person is very important; the man you are dating, for instance. He claims he makes $50,000 a year as an undercover agent, but beyond that he is vague. If he is telling the truth, he may be quite an extraordinary fellow; but if he is telling a lie, marrying him is likely to bring monumental problems.

So here stands Jesus before you, claiming to be the Son of God. If He is, you have found the unique person of the universe. If He isn't, he is just another nut.

If He is the Son of God, you had better dedicate your soul, your body, your mind, your life to Him; but if He isn't, you would do well to have nothing more to do with Christ or the Christian religion.

If He is what He claims to be, you can accept all of His teachings and live wholeheartedly by them; if not, you'll have to write them off as a bad joke.

If He is the Son of God, the gospel record is a true and accurate account; if not, it is an elaborate and cruel hoax.

If He is the Son of God He can be your Savior for all eternity; if He isn't, He is a self-deluded megalomaniac.

You can't suspend your judgment; the claim is too startling, the issues are too vital, the stakes are too high. You can't say "Wait and see" because you'll pass this way only once.

The facts are in. The decision is yours.

INTERPRETIVE COMMENTS

The Jewish Sanhedrin had no authority to execute anyone; only the Roman government could do that. If they wanted Jesus put to death, the Jewish leaders had to convince Pilate that Jesus was a threat to the Roman government. So in order to get Him to incriminate Himself, they asked Him, "If you are the Christ, tell us" (v. 67). Jesus saw through their strategy and refused to answer. He did, however, make another claim—a claim that the Roman authorities would not understand, but that the Jewish leaders would understand only too well: "But from now on the Son of man shall be seated at the right hand of the power of God" (v. 69). Jesus was referring to the words of the prophet Daniel, who spoke of a coming divine-human being called the Son of man (Dan. 7:13). The implications were far-reaching and startling, so they asked

Him point-blank, "Are you the Son of God, then?" (v. 70a). Without really saying yes, Jesus affirmed it (v. 70b). The leaders settled for a lesser victory than they had hoped for. Although they had elicited no confession which would incriminate Him before Pilate, they believed they had convicted Him of blasphemy—an offense which they could use to turn public opinion against Him.

Today controversy flares up from time to time about the literal nature of the phrase, *Son of God*.

Those who take one point of view say that Jesus was a son of God, as all people who are obedient and loving are sons and daughters of God. It is not necessary, they say, to believe in a literal virgin birth and a divine nature. Jesus was simply a person who lived more completely as a child of God than most of us do.

Those who take the other point of view refer to the scriptural stories of Jesus' conception, indicating that the writers of the Gospels believed whole-heartedly in the virgin birth and the literal sonship of Christ. Jesus, they say, is unique, one of a kind.

DISCUSSION QUESTIONS

1. Do you believe that Jesus is literally the Son of God, via the virgin birth? If not, what do you believe the phrase, *Son of God* means? How did the writers of the Gospels and Epistles understand the term?

2. How important is it to believe in the virgin birth? Is it necessary for salvation? If Jesus was not the unique, literal Son of God, what does this indicate about the reliability of Luke's Gospel? What

83

does it imply about the meaning of the cross? About the integrity of Mary?

3. What do we think today about anyone who claims to be divine or divinely-inspired? Do you think for a moment that these people could be right? Why would they make such claims? Perhaps our answers to these questions may help us understand why Jesus was hesitant during most of His ministry to promote the concept of His deity. Why was Jesus more willing to say near the end of His life that He was the Son of God?

4. If Jesus is the unique Son of God in the full sense, in what way are other people children of God? Can unbelievers be called children of God in any sense of the term? What qualifies a person to be called a child of God? (See John 1:12, 13.)

20

Being Born Again

"How can a man be born when he is old?"
(John 3:4)

Scripture for study: John 3:1-8

"I'd give anything if I could do it over again."

You have heard it—and perhaps said it, but it is too late to change the past. Those words and deeds can't be erased. What is done is done, and to try to change it is futile.

"I've tried to change, but I just can't."

You have heard it—and perhaps said it. But no matter how hard you try, you can't seem to control that explosive temper or stop smoking or change your attitude toward the opposite sex or conquer your anxiety.

You need a fresh start. But it seems impossible, because you can't turn back the time machine to the moment of your birth.

Take heart, said Jesus. A fresh start really is possible. You can indeed be born again.

The past can be erased. You can be born "of water" (v. 5). The guilt can be washed away. The black smudges on your soul are soluble. Your personal history need no longer be a dark shadow which stalks every present moment. God can make you clean again. He can give you a fresh start.

As the past can be erased, so the present can be revitalized. You can also be born "of the Spirit" (v. 5). You don't have to rely on your own weak will. God's Spirit is there to take over your spirit. His Spirit will give you a new hope, a new ambition, a new joy. The future isn't a hopeless blob of the impossible after all.

Yes, says Jesus, you can have a fresh start. You can be born again. And this time you will never die.

INTERPRETIVE COMMENTS

Nicodemus was a Pharisee and a member of the Sanhedrin (John 7:50), the seventy-member congress of the Jews whose authority was now limited to religious matters. Nicodemus came to Jesus under cover of darkness, probably to avoid being seen by his friends. (Imagine a member of the Ku Klux Klan stopping in to have a chat with the local leader of B'nai B'rith!) Somehow, all his theological training had not satisfied his deep spiritual needs, and he sensed that Jesus might have the answer. Unlike most of his colleagues, he was open to the truth and was not afraid to open the windows of his life to God's fresh air.

Nicodemus appears to have remained a secret believer until he spoke out (still rather timidly) on Jesus' behalf before the Sanhedrin (John 7:50). Then, after it was seemingly too late, he and another secret disciple, Joseph of Arimathea, came "out of the closet" and gave proper burial to Jesus' body (John 19:38-40).

The key words of verse 3 can be translated either "born anew" or "born from above." Most prefer the former translation. Birth can be viewed either from the father's side (beget) or from the mother's side (bear). The former is used here.

Two factors are involved in this process, says Jesus: "Unless one is born of water and the Spirit, he cannot enter the kingdom of God" (v. 5).

Being "born of water" might be interpreted as baptism, but the physical act of baptism is too simple, too easily abused to be in itself accountable for the great miracle described here. Rather, being "born of water" refers to the inward cleansing that baptism symbolizes. It implies the forgiveness that sweeps away the old and thus makes possible a new start.

"Born of the Spirit" implies the activity of God which transforms the inner being, a kind of "divine conception" that produces a new life. As a father and mother is to the life of the body, so the Spirit is to the life of the soul. It would be a mistake, however, to say that this new birth is limited to the inner self. It begins there, but from that point begins to affect all other areas of life, creating a desire for new truth, strength for moral decisions, mobilization for service, and sensitivity to the needs of others. In short, it is an answer to the prayer of David, "Create in me a clean heart, O God, and put a new and right spirit within me" (Ps. 51:10).

DISCUSSION QUESTIONS

1. Once thought of as a term common only to raving evangelistic fundamentalists, "born again" has suddenly become a respectable term. Much of

this change in attitude has been attributed to such people as Jimmy Carter and to such converts as Chuck Colson and Eldridge Cleaver. In what ways is this public prominence beneficial to Christianity? In what ways can it be harmful?

2. When people like Larry Flynt, publisher of *Hustler* magazine, claim to have been born again, people are skeptical. Is this skepticism justified? Should we immediately accept these professed converts as brothers and sisters in Christ, or should we say, "Let's wait and see if their conversion is real"? What attitude is most beneficial to the Christian growth of the new convert?

3. The term *born again* implies major change. What changes take place? What changes do not take place? Are these changes immediate? Are some of these changes long-range? If little or no change is apparent, is it probable that no "born again" experience actually took place?

4. Jesus' words to Nicodemus are interpreted differently by various Christian groups. At what points do you agree with this author's interpretation? At what points do you disagree?

21

Breaking Down
Social Barriers

*"How is it that you, a Jew, ask a drink of me,
a woman of Samaria?" (John 4:9)*

Scripture for study: John 4:7-9

There were at least five reasons why Jesus should
not have spoken to the person at the well. That person was 1) female, 2) of the wrong nationality, 3)
of the wrong religion, 4) divorced, and 5) living
with a man without benefit of marriage.

Jesus, in one act of cordiality, swept across the
barriers of 1) sex, 2) nationality, 3) religion, 4)
reputation, and 5) character.

She may have been brazenly flaunting the moral
standards of her community, but Jesus saw a woman
struggling for a sense of personal satisfaction and
worth. She may have been adhering to a faulty
theology, but Jesus saw a person craving a genuine
spiritual experience. Here was a human being with
real needs, and Jesus asked no more than that. He
initiated a conversation that led not only to her
conversion but also to the conversion of others in
the community.

Have you ever tried to strike up a conversation
with a long-haired youth while waiting for your car

at the garage? With the seventy-five-year-old painted redhead in the next airplane seat? With the fat girl across the aisle in your classroom? With the black man who shares a bench with you at the shopping mall? With the pregnant woman with two missing front teeth and three small children clamoring behind you at the checkout line? With the new kid on the block that everybody says is weird?

Try it. The protocol for Jesus' kingdom is a bit different from that of the social register.

INTERPRETIVE COMMENTS

A quick look at a map of Palestine will show that the direct route between Judea and Galilee lay through the area of Samaria, but most Jews chose to go out of their way, through Perea. Jesus showed a definite neglect of protocol by walking through "enemy" territory. Sychar is generally associated with the modern village of Askar, which is about a mile north of Jacob's well. The traditional site of Jacob's tomb is about halfway between Askar and the well.

The bitter feelings between Jews and Samaritans were based on both ethnic and religious grounds. Samaritans were of part Israelite ancestry and part some other nationality. At the time of the captivity of Israel in 722 B.C., the Babylonians deported most of the upper class Israelites (by Sargon's count, 27,290), hence the "lost ten tribes" of Israel. Then the Babylonians replaced these people with other captured and displaced peoples who intermarried with the remaining children of Israel. Their children were the "half-breed" Samaritans. The Jewish religious heritage of these people also came to a halt, as they accepted as their Scripture only the Pentateuch, the five books of Moses. Instead of worshiping at Jerusalem, they worshiped at Mount Gerizim. Like many others before and since, their similarities were ignored and their differences were exaggerated until the situation became almost intolerable.

People who have studied that culture tell us that it was odd for the woman to come to draw water at that time of day. Most women did this task in the cool of the evening, when they turned a household necessity into a social amenity by exchanging the news of the day. Perhaps this woman had been cold-shouldered out of such pleasantries (after all, she was a potential threat to every woman in town) and preferred to come when she could do so without experiencing the sting of social rejection. Jesus' friendliness in this situation was audacious indeed.

DISCUSSION QUESTIONS

1. Every social grouping, no matter how large or small, has its outcasts—those who in one way or another do not live up to the norms of the group. Outcast status can be determined by race, nationality, income, marital status, conduct, or any number of other factors. Who do you believe are the outcasts of American society as a whole? Of your city? Of your neighborhood? Of your third-grade classroom? Of your office staff? Of your neighborhood over-the-back-fence gang? Of your senior class? Of your church? (Yes—of your church. Are there any "second-class citizens" in your church?)

2. In what ways do we sometimes let other peo-

ple know that they are not "our kind"? How do groups ostracize people? How do individuals do it? Do we try to disguise our intentions? If so, does it mean we are ashamed of them? Do we really fool anybody?

3. It is possible that the woman at the well came early in the day to avoid being reminded of her status in the community. In what other ways do people try to compensate or deal with the problem of being shut out of normal friendships? Are these methods effective?

4. How should we as Christians deal with the outsider, the strange one, the person with the bad reputation, the one who doesn't quite fit in with our group? How should we treat that person in the Sunday school class? After church on Sunday morning? While riding home from work together? At the laundromat?

22

Inner Resources

"Sir, you have nothing to draw with, and the well is deep; where do you get that living water?" (John 4:11)

Scripture for study: John 4:10-15

Water is life. Without food an average human can live as long as thirty days; without water, only a few days.

Water is cleansing. No better all-purpose substance has ever been found for washing away the accumulated grime of everyday living.

Water is pleasure. It splashes and sparkles, renews and refreshes, comforts and cools.

Life without water is first of all, grubby and pleasureless; then painful and deathly.

It isn't only the body that needs water, implies Jesus; the soul also needs a certain kind of water in order to thrive. Like the body, it can become parched and crusty.

The soul needs a certain kind of water for cleansing. The inner person, like the outer one, becomes gritty with foreign matter in the course of everyday living.

The soul needs a certain kind of water for pleasure. Those things that excite the body often leave the soul unmoved, empty, and barren.

And where does one obtain this water of life? It is available from only one source: the Creator of H_2O. The same God who brings you streams, lakes, oceans, and sparkling glasses of water brings you the living water that bubbles up in the inner being.

INTERPRETIVE COMMENTS

Jesus, in His conversation with the Samaritan woman at the well, quickly turned the conversation around. First He *asked* for water, but within a minute He *offered* water. The guest suddenly became the host.

The woman was skeptical, and she said so; but her response went beyond the mere mechanics of water-drawing. "Are you greater than our father Jacob who gave us the well?" she asked (v. 12). This question would seem to indicate an inward thirst as well as a bodily one; the woman was indeed searching for someone greater than Abraham. She desperately needed someone to put her life back together again.

"Living water" (v. 10) means, first of all, fresh, flowing water, as opposed to stagnant water. In the Old Testament it is also a metaphor for divine activity in people. God is called the fountain of living waters (Jer. 2:13), and Zechariah prophesied that living waters would flow out from Jerusalem (Zech. 14:8).

The woman failed to understand the symbolism of the "spring of water welling up to eternal life" (v. 14). We are in a position to interpret that promise both from the perspective of the Old Testament symbolism and from the perspective of Pentecost. The Holy Spirit, which Jesus promised "will be in you" (John 14:17), is an inexhaustible source of strength, peace, and joy. The Spirit of Christ initiates the new life, then continues to bubble up within that life. He will continue to do so through physical death and into eternity.

DISCUSSION QUESTIONS

1. Suggest some modern-day "women (and men) at the well"—people who a) seemingly lived exciting and even "swinging" lives; but who b) inwardly were empty, desperately thirsty for some kind of meaningful existence; and c) found Christ to be the answer to these deep inner needs. Many of these may be well-known personalities whose conversions have attracted widespread attention. Others are "nobodies," known only to a small circle of relatives and friends. Discuss how their experiences with Christ may have been similar to that of the woman at the well, especially in reference to the three points mentioned above.

2. What personality traits might cause a person to run through five marriages in succession? To change jobs with the same kind of rapidity? To move constantly from one place to another? Do these behavior patterns indicate a certain kind of inner hunger? How can Christ meet these kinds of needs?

3. Sometimes salvation is spoken of as a once-for-all experience. Discuss the long-range implications of "a spring of water welling up to eternal life" (v. 14). What might this imply for the woman's lifestyle? About her concept of true happiness? About her long-range goals in life?

23

Evidence Worth Believing

"What sign do you do, that we may see, and believe you?" (John 6:30)

Scripture for study: John 6:25-34

People are always looking for a "sign"—some objective evidence, some proof that can be seen, heard, or felt.

That is not all bad. When someone claims to have seen a flying saucer, we want some kind of proof. When a scientist says he has developed a pill which will cure cancer, the Food and Drug Administration wants to see the evidence. When a freshman says, "I'm a great basketball player," the coach says, "Prove it." When an advertisement says, "We have discovered a miracle drug which will cure baldness," we say, "I'll believe it when I see it."

Jesus' onlookers had every right to ask for evidence. After all, the claims made by His followers were outrageous. They said He was the Messiah foretold by the prophets. They even said He was divine, the Son of God.

In their search for evidence, however, the critics made a few serious errors. For one thing, they were looking for the wrong kind of evidence. They were looking only for the physical. They wanted an instant replay of the miracle of the loaves and the fishes or some kind of modern manna machine.

People make the same kind of mistakes today. They evaluate religious leaders by the miraculous healings they perform, by the cathedrals they build, by the crowds they attract, or by the contributions they accumulate.

The second mistake made by Jesus' critics was that they had decided beforehand that they weren't going to believe the evidence anyway. In truth, the evidence was already indisputable. They and their friends had already witnessed miracles. Their only reaction to Jesus' healing of the man with the withered hand had been to criticize Him for doing it on Sunday.

It is fine to ask for evidence. In fact, we must demand it. But let's 1) ask for the right kind, and 2) be prepared to accept the consequences.

INTERPRETIVE COMMENTS

There was a rabbinical rule in Christ's time that if a man claimed to be a prophet but was not yet recognized as such, he was to give a sign or wonder. If he succeeded, he was to be listened to, but if he failed, he was to be ignored.

Jesus had given such a sign on the hillside, but the people said, in effect, "So what? Moses also fed the people in the wilderness. That doesn't make you any more than he was" (see v. 31).

Jesus responded by pointing out that it was God, not Moses, who performed the miracles in the wilderness, and that God is now prepared to feed

His people with the bread which can give life to all (v. 33). One would think that by then the people would have begun to see the deeper meaning of Jesus' words, but they did not. "Lord, give us this bread always," they said (v. 34), still bound by the physical sense of the word. Finally Jesus said plainly, "I am the bread of life" (v. 35). The conversation went on and on, back and forth, for thirty more verses, but to no avail. John describes the conclusion of the discussion with some of the saddest words ever recorded in Scripture: "After this many of his disciples drew back and no longer went about with him" (John 6:66). Neither miracles nor logic will do any good unless a person has the will to believe.

DISCUSSION QUESTIONS

1. What is the difference between normal, healthy skepticism and the unhealthy kind? What are the characteristics of each?

2. The Bible says, on one hand, that love "believes all things" (I Cor. 13:7); but on the other hand, exhorts Christians to "test the spirits to see whether they are of God" (I John 4:1). How can we achieve a balance which will do both? How can we be cautious about strange teachings without at the same time blocking out new outpourings of God's Spirit? How can we be receptive to God's leading without being duped by false teaching?

3. What criteria should we use to "test the spirits"? When a new movement arises, for instance, should we evaluate the lives of its leaders? The clarity of its written teachings? The biblical nature of its theology? The responsibility it shows in so-

liciting and distributing finances? The claims it may make to be the "only" way?

5. Are our decisions to believe or disbelieve based on the evidence alone? Evaluate the statement, "Many young people who reject the gospel say they are doing so because they have an intellectual problem, but in reality they just do not want to change their lifestyle."

24

Becoming Liberated

"How is it that you say, 'You will be made free'?" (John 8:33)

Scripture for study: John 8:31-38

"We have never been in bondage to any one," they said (v. 33). Therefore they saw no reason to be liberated.

"No one is more enslaved," someone has said, "than he who imagines himself to be free."

The last one to know that he is an alcoholic is usually the alcoholic himself. The same is often true of a person addicted to drugs, or to tobacco, or to excessive food. Compulsive gamblers, shoplifters, child-beaters, wife-beaters, and husband-beaters are often the last to realize that their impulses are out of control.

Other kinds of bondage are more subtle. The people talking to Jesus were presumably free of these more flagrant types of bondage. Yet they were prisoners of an iron-clad system of legalism. Virtually every hour of their lives was dictated by thousands of dos and don'ts.

The person enslaved by racial bigotry says, "I don't hate them. Some of them are my best friends."

And he really believes it. The chronic complainer sincerely believes he is giving constructive criticism. The compulsive shopper believes he really needs everything he buys.

Sin, said Jesus, is a terrible tyrant (see v. 34). It takes away the freedom of the will, clouds the mind, befuddles the decision-making process, and makes accurate self-evaluation all but impossible.

The solution? The truth. The truth about God, about the Spirit, about the Son, about ourselves, about right and wrong, about heaven and hell, about forgiveness and grace.

When we know the truth, we will be truly free.

INTERPRETIVE COMMENTS

Even though becoming a Christian involves an experience of being "born again" (see John 3:1-8), this inner transformation does not automatically bring complete freedom. Old habits and hangups will still persist, limiting personal development and Christian growth, keeping the individual from achieving his full potential. Growth is necessary for freedom.

There is a difference between outward freedom and inward freedom. An individual, for instance, may be free to worship God according to the dictates of his own conscience, but he may be so inwardly bound that he cannot worship anyone greater than himself. One may be free to contribute ample resources to any number of causes, but be such a slave to greed that he finds it impossible to part with any of it. A person may know in his mind that it is okay for him to go to a good movie, but his strict childhood training continues to bind him even as an adult.

Moving from slavery to freedom involves, according to this passage, five steps:

1) Believing. Jesus was talking here to the Jews "who had believed in him" (v. 31a).

2) Continuing in Jesus' word (v. 31b). This implies a long-range program of both learning and obeying Jesus' teachings.

3) Becoming Jesus' disciples (v. 31c), the natural outgrowth of continuing in His word. Disciples follow their master, learning by example as well as by word.

4) Knowing the truth (v. 32a). Being a disciple rather than a dabbler leads to a full comprehension of the truth.

5) Becoming free (v. 32b). Free from what? Free from the trap of sin, from bad memories of the past, from the legalism of a certain religious heritage, from enslaving personal habits, from racial prejudice, from long-standing personal grudges, from persistent superstition (black cats and the thirteenth floor).

These bondages aren't broken easily. They can be loosed only after a long, intense, and persistent discipleship. But when one truly learns the truth from Him who is the Truth, all things become possible.

DISCUSSION QUESTIONS

1. Young people often say they "want to be free." In what ways do they express this desire? In what respects can this be a healthy attitude? In what respects can it be an unhealthy one? Do they neces-

sarily want as much freedom as they say they do?

2. Some criminals converted in prison have said that they felt more free inside prison than when they were outside prison walls. What do you suppose they mean by that?

3. The meditation on this passage suggests a number of ways in which people are inwardly bound. Name a number of additional ways in which people are prevented by inner compulsions from living productive and happy lives. Are all of these necessarily caused by sin? Can all of them be somehow cured by a knowledge of the truth?

4. In what ways have our religious traditions wrongfully taken away certain freedoms? Do you feel that your own tradition has been unnecessarily strict in the matter of Sunday observance? Dress codes? Entertainment? Sexual morality? Money matters? Discuss Galatians 3–4 in light of these questions. Pressures were being placed on the Christians at Galatia to return to the legalism of Judaism, which would have taken away their new-found freedom in Christ. Are we in danger of that today? Or have we gone to the opposite extreme?

25

The Cause of
Sickness and Handicaps

"Who sinned, this man or his parents, that he was born blind?" (John 9:2)

Scripture for study: John 9

As if it weren't bad enough being blind, this poor man had to listen to the whispered speculations about what sin and whose sin it was that made him that way.

It was common in ancient times to believe that physical ailments were a punishment for sin and that good health was a sign of God's approval. (Consider the testimony of Job's three friends.) Thus people who were well became susceptible to spiritual pride, and people who were sick or handicapped were apt to become both mentally and spiritually depressed.

Jesus ventured the opinion that the man's condition had nothing to do with sin, rather that his blindness fit into a plan that would ultimately give glory to God.

But old falsehoods die slowly. Some well-meaning disciples still teach that heart attacks, arthritis, and appendicitis are sent by God to mold your character—implying, of course, that your character obviously needs some improvement.

Others say that Jesus has already paid the price of your physical healing on the cross, and all you must do is claim it by faith. If you are not healed, it is obvious you don't really have faith.

The Bible does not promise physical healing on demand. God will not be coerced or manipulated by even the strongest of Christians. Even Paul had to learn to live with the thorn in his flesh. "My grace is sufficient for you, for my power is made perfect in weakness," said God (II Cor. 12:9). God's people certainly don't have to feel guilty about not being well.

INTERPRETIVE COMMENTS

This miracle is significant for a number of reasons. For one thing, Jesus showed that concern for people's needs is more important than adherence to outmoded customs. Jesus denied that the man's blindness was caused by some sin committed by the man's parents or by the man himself, a belief widely held in Jewish tradition. Jesus made a small mud pack of dust and saliva and applied it to the blind man's eyes, thus disobeying the rules which forbade applying saliva to the eyes and working on the Sabbath. Some of these beliefs, especially the one regarding the relationship of guilt and sickness, were imposing a cruel hardship on those who were already suffering a physical handicap.

Second, Jesus demonstrated the importance of a person's involvement in his own cure. Jesus asked the blind man to wash in the pool of Siloam (a site which has to this day retained that name). Since

Jesus did not tell the man why he should do it; this involved some faith. Even today, most miracles involve the active participation of those who need the miracle.

Third, the miracle was a living illustration of the person of Christ: "I am the light of the world" (v. 5). He was the light-giver on all levels.

DISCUSSION QUESTIONS

1. How common is it today to believe that one's good fortune is connected to one's righteous life? Is this believed more strongly in religious circles or in non-religious circles?

2. Those who believe Jesus died for our diseases as well as for our sins quote Isaiah 53:5: "But he was wounded for our transgressions, he was bruised for our iniquities; upon him was the chastisement that made us whole, and with his stripes we are healed." Is this really what that passage means? Do any other biblical passages substantiate this teaching? Is it found in the epistles?

3. The Book of Job tells how Job's three friends came to visit him for the purpose of giving comfort. What was their theory about the reason for Job's misfortunes? What did Job eventually call his friends? Did Job ever receive a full explanation of why all those terrible things happened to him? Did Job ever find it necessary to repent of some sin which supposedly brought about his problems? Do Job's three friends have any modern counterparts?

4. Is it true that those who give generously to God's work will, in return, receive generous financial rewards later in life? Do you know of great saints who die almost penniless? Do you know of

unscrupulous rascals who die at a ripe old age in their luxurious oceanside condominiums? Is either riches or poverty a reflection on piety?

26

Spending Money

*"Why was this ointment not sold for three
hundred denarii and given to the poor?"*
(John 12:5)

Scripture for study: John 12:1-8

Questions similar to the one above are still being
asked today.

"Why spend billions to send men to the moon
while there are so many problems on earth which
we have not solved?"

"Instead of spending $5 million on a fancy church,
why not give that money to missions?"

"It's ridiculous to spend that much money for a
sculpture in the park while just a few blocks away
thousands of people live in substandard housing."

"Wealthy people could solve a lot of the world's
problems if they would just spread their money
around."

"Instead of exchanging Christmas gifts this year,
let's give the money we save to some benevolent
cause."

"It's a shame that people spend so much money
for funeral flowers that wilt in just a few days. It

would be better to contribute that money to some worthwhile fund."

These proposals are of varying degrees of merit. All of them are somewhat different from the biblical incident, in which the ointment is used as a personal tribute to Christ Himself. Yet the principal conflict is much the same: general basic needs versus special personal tributes. The first is intensely practical; the second is often impractical. The first fills immediate needs; the second fills long-range needs. The first deals mostly with survival; the second deals mostly with civilization and culture. The first fills the need for food and clothing; the second fills the need for recognition and accomplishment. The first fills the needs of the body; the second fills the needs of the soul and mind.

We will not attempt to resolve all these matters here; but we will point out that, in this biblical incident at least, Jesus opted for the personal/impractical solution.

INTERPRETIVE COMMENTS

This story is to be distinguished from that recorded in Luke 7:36-50, in which a sinful woman came to the house of Simon the Pharisee, where Jesus was dining. There, without regard for the other guests, she wept bitterly, her tears falling on Jesus' feet, which she proceeded to wipe with her tears and to anoint with oil. The incident recorded by John involved Jesus' good friend Mary, who lived with Martha and Lazarus at Bethany. Martha, no doubt, was busy serving the meal (see Luke 10:38, 40).

Judas objected to this expenditure, at least partly because he, as the treasurer, occasionally dipped his hand into the group's resources. Such an objection was not limited to thieves, however, since in the incident of the sinful woman it was the disciples as a whole (Matt. 26:8) and some of the other people (Mark 14:4) who questioned the expenditure.

Mary's act was a spontaneous outpouring of love. It may not have been a very practical one, since the ointment was worth many days' wages, but it expressed the depths of her devotion as nothing else could. As Jesus said of the other woman who did the same thing, "She has done a beautiful thing" (Matt. 26:10).

Dramatic acts of devotion are often difficult for "outsiders" to understand. Non-Christians find tithing to be stupid (except as an income tax deduction), and small boys consider their older brothers who buy flowers for girls to be incomprehensibly silly. Similarly, Judas could view Mary's sacrifice for Jesus only with utter dismay.

DISCUSSION QUESTIONS

1. Discuss the issue of spending the money for an expensive church versus giving the money to the poor. Is spending money for the church a kind of ego trip for the pastor and parishioners? Is it a way of memorializing themselves? Is it true that a more beautiful building will attract more people, and that a growing church will, over the years, be able to raise more money for benevolent causes? Can the new church be justified on the basis that it is being built for the glory of God, and that God

deserves the best? If $500,000 is withdrawn from the price of the church, will that amount actually be given to the poor? Which will be seen as the best investment fifty years from now? Did not our forefathers face the same kind of decision regarding the church we are worshiping in now, and are we not pleased that they went forward in building it?

2. Discuss one of the other issues alluded to in the first section of this chapter, pursuing it in a manner similar to that above. Perhaps your church or community is facing a similar dilemma.

3. Part of the ransom Randolph Hearst paid to the kidnappers of his daughter Patty was to give away $1 million in food for the poor. Did this act have very much of a long-term (or even short-term) effect on the poor community?

4. As families we sometimes must make decisions similar to the others raised by this lesson. Should the husband buy a bouquet of flowers, which will wilt in a few days, or should he buy a U-joint for the bathroom sink? Should we go out to a restaurant to celebrate a special event, or should we use that money to pay off some bills? Should we buy a piano, which is a kind of luxury, or should we buy a sofa, which is more of a necessity? Should we increase our church pledge when we are already deeply in debt? On what basis can such decisions be made? Can they be made on practicality alone? What personal and human implications must be considered?